© 2015 fassforward Consulting Group
Author: Gavin McMahon
Art Direction: Brandon Chin
Layout & Graphic Design: Ray Vella, Eugene Yoon

*"People have Chocolate Conversations when they are talking past each other and have completely different points of view, while believing, they're on the same page."*

–Rose Fass, *The Chocolate Conversation*

# THE WAY WE'VE LEARNED TO COMMUNICATE IS WRONG.

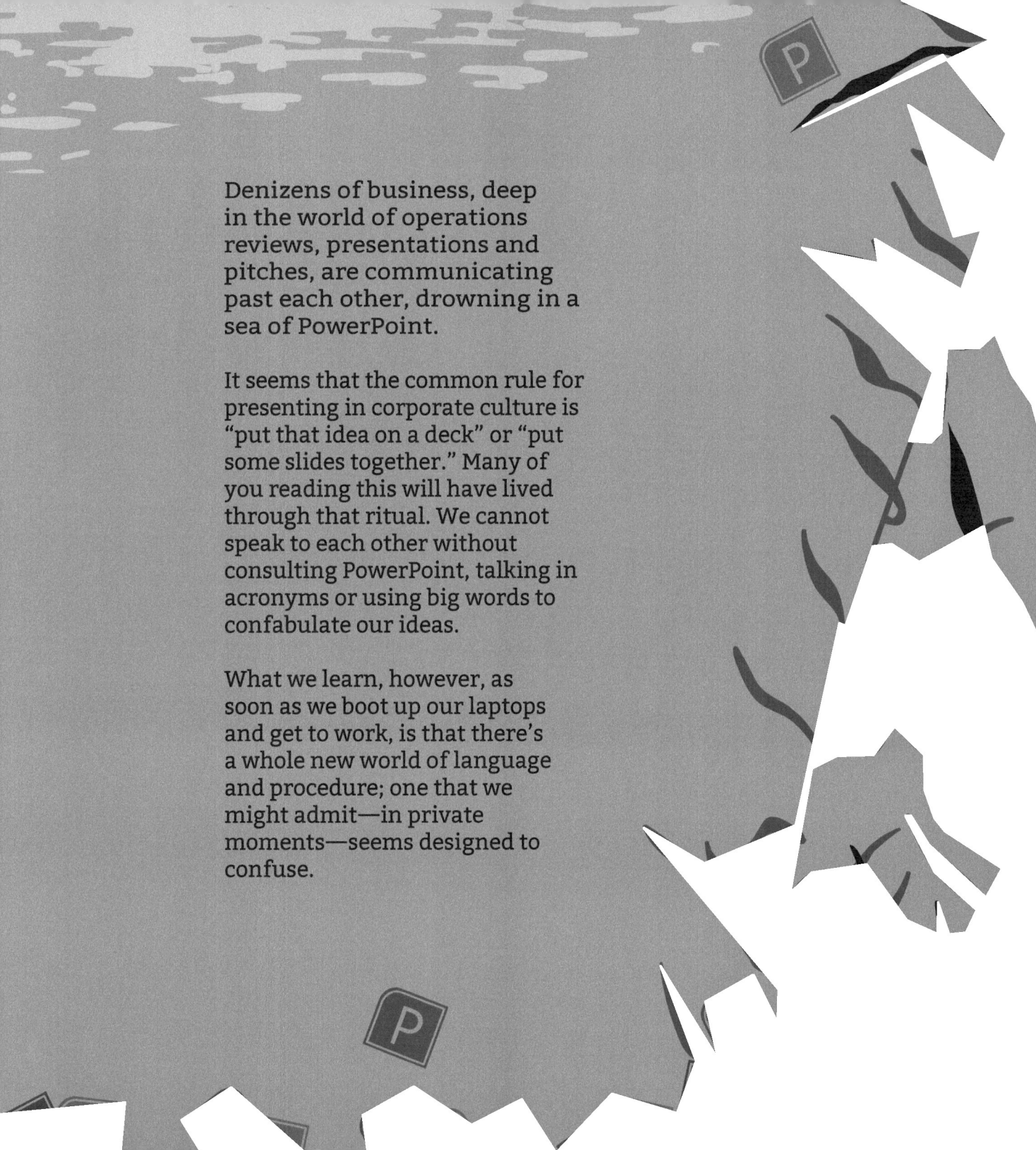

Denizens of business, deep in the world of operations reviews, presentations and pitches, are communicating past each other, drowning in a sea of PowerPoint.

It seems that the common rule for presenting in corporate culture is "put that idea on a deck" or "put some slides together." Many of you reading this will have lived through that ritual. We cannot speak to each other without consulting PowerPoint, talking in acronyms or using big words to confabulate our ideas.

What we learn, however, as soon as we boot up our laptops and get to work, is that there's a whole new world of language and procedure; one that we might admit—in private moments—seems designed to confuse.

# YOU HAVE A CHOICE.

*You can choose door #1*

Door #1 is to reskill yourself with PowerPoint. You will learn the arcane language of leverage and synergy, master buzzwords like "hyper-growth" and "ecosystem," and absorb acronyms like EBITDA and ARPU. You will join the herd.

*Or you can choose door #2*

Door #2 is a return to your roots.
A return to the lessons learned in
your childhood and to a way of
communicating that comes naturally.
The path through Door #2 requires
a maverick soul and a streak of
independence, but the reward is greater
— an ability to communicate more
clearly, to persuade and convince,
and to develop a hard skill for the 21st
century.

Door #2 is a journey aimed at
unlearning the acquired jargon in your
system and cleansing your palate of
corporate BS. It is the acquisition of a
complementary type of literacy —
a visual one.

We've Been Having **Conversations**

For **A Long Time**

To understand why this is relevant now more than ever,
we must go back 2 million years.

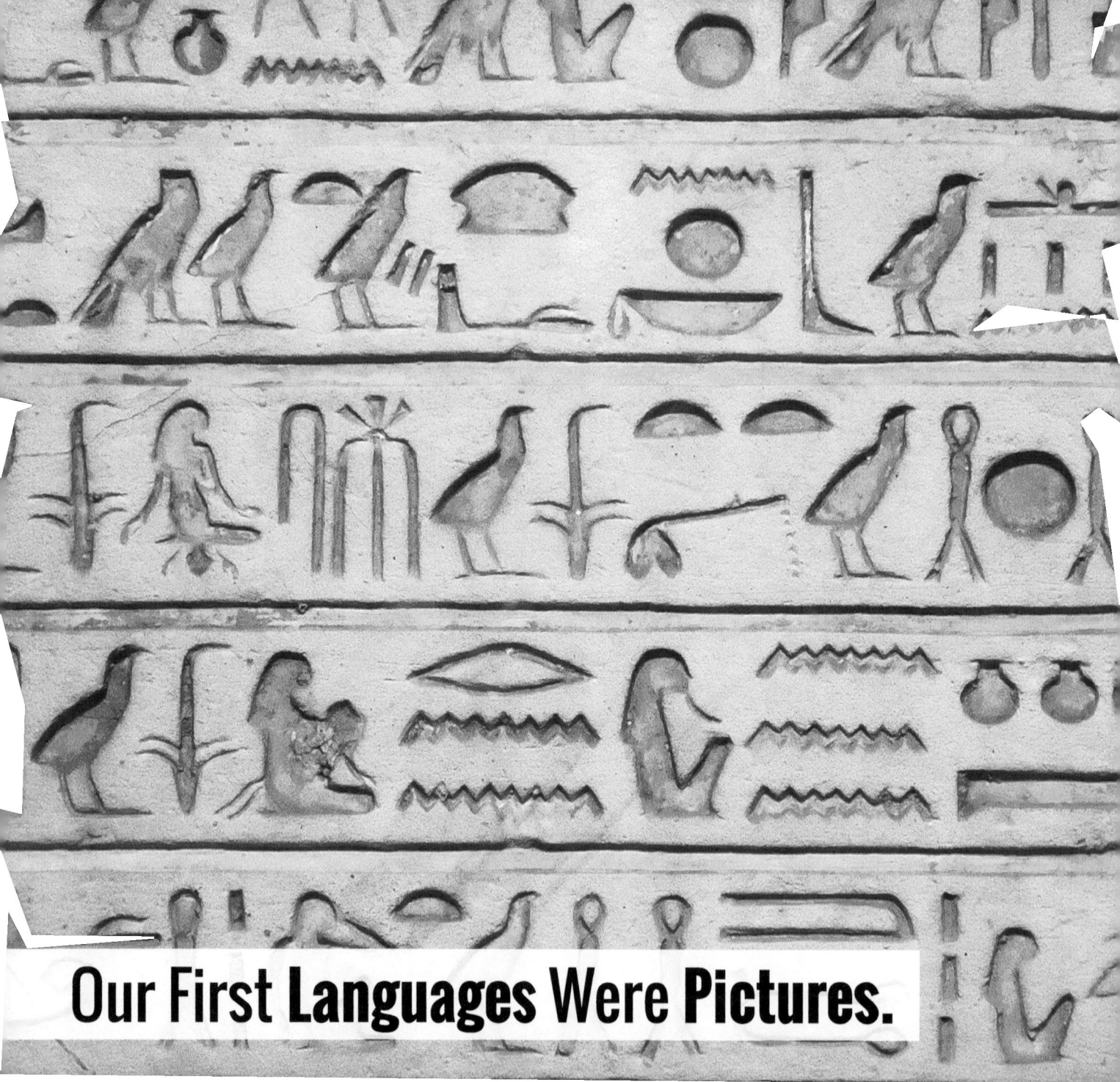

Our First **Languages** Were **Pictures.**

That's how long we've been talking (or at least grunting) to each other. What started out as grunts and gestures quickly evolved into words and language. Our first "written" languages were pictures—Cuneiform script and Egyptian hieroglyphs. It was a natural way to record our stories, our history, and our laws, to govern and to fuel trade. It was a way for us to make meaning.

A blip on the calendar later, in relative terms, the "art" of speaking was codified. By the time of Socrates, Aristotle and Plato, oral tradition not only had the framework and rules of rhetoric, but oratory had become a revered skill.

By the middle ages, artful communication, in the form of pictures or words, was in the hands of a few. Books were laboriously written and illuminated by religious orders. Those privileged few in the literate class—the polymaths, the geniuses and the creators, like Da Vinci and Galileo—stood out. The rest of us, from the wealthiest to the poorest of people, were illiterate. Literacy wasn't even a rich man's game, it was a specialist's. That began to change when we had tools and applied mass-production (printing) to writing. The invention of the printing press in 1453 led to the first publishing house, the Cambridge Univ. Press formed in 1534.

Declining costs and wider availability allowed communication and literacy to spread from the hands (and mouths) of specialists and experts to a wider audience. By the 18th century, communication had evolved from a cottage industry into a business. Lloyd's List was started in 1734, the Pittsburgh Post Gazette in 1786, and the Wall St. Journal in 1889— all forebears of the media industry today.

Business Communicated.

The invention of the telegraph, along with the spread of the rail system in Europe and America, not only meant that goods moved faster, but that information moved faster, as well. In 1855, Western Union formed, and quickly followed the rail boom to connect metropolitan areas all over the United States.

Less than 11 years later, the first stock ticker was demonstrated. In 1874, Alexander Graham Bell's invention of the telephone resulted in the incorporation of the Bell Patent Association, turning into AT&T a few years later. The business of communication was maturing fast and had no plans to stop.

And language **changed.**

While early tools shaped how business communicated, the style in which it communicated was shaped by the military. They returned from service in World War II to a post-war boom that changed how we work.

The hierarchical command and control structures you see in most corporations today have roots in the military. **Our language changed.** We did things *ASAP*. Businesses had a *mission* and a *strategy* and their salespeople had *territories*. Tiger teams tackled *snafus in the field* or headquarters, while marketers *positioned* products.

# { Tools shape the way we think. }

In that post-war boom, new tools spread and continued to shape how we communicated. Memos were formal, dictated and typed. Reports were written. White papers were authored.

This has lead to generations in business — boomers, X and Y — who prize verbal and written literacy in the way Greeks and Romans prized oratory. Advancement and authority depend on a person's ability to write reports and turn a phrase.

The ability to draw and to capture or explain ideas visually isn't in the mainstream of business. Doodling is viewed as a hobby for the absent-minded. The first computers didn't help either, as they weren't much more than word processors. Even the first graphical packages weren't very easy on the eyes. Although this is slowly changing, resistance to visualization is still the norm.

# And that's a problem.

SUGAR

**Information** is exploding.

So much communication, from the nonverbal cues in a negotiation to the billboard for your latest marketing campaign, is visual. Mobile technology is accelerating this fact. Video cameras that were the province of well-heeled hobbyists and professionals two decades ago, now are in everyone's hands. Anyone can be a media creator and anyone can be a journalist. More than half of us have smart phones and are Googling, Instagramming, Tweeting and Facebooking non-stop.

Information is exploding. We've recorded and produced more information in the last two years than we did in the previous two million. We're not just swapping out hard drives and moving to the cloud; we're inventing new words like Exabyte and Yottabyte to quantify the abundance of information today.

As the world wades in and produces more 'Big Data' professions, Data Scientists and Data Visualizers are emerging to make sense of it all. Startups fueled this growth in visual content. Google acquired Youtube for $1.65 Billion in 2006, Facebook acquired Instagram for $1 Billion in 2012 and was spurned by Snapchat for $3 Billion. Money talks, and it's speaking pictures.

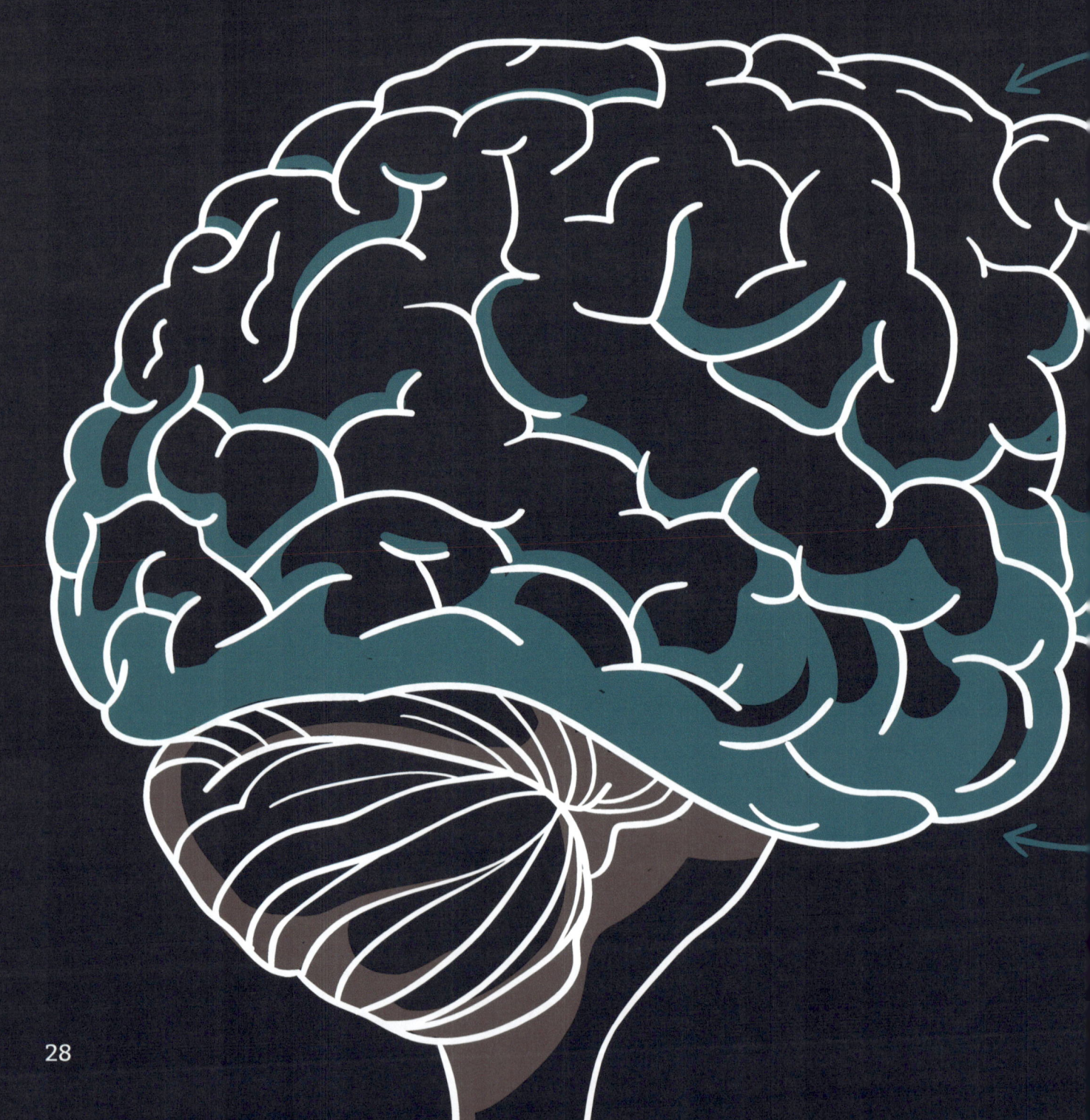

*MIT neuroscientists found that the brain can identify images seen for as little as 13 milliseconds.*

*Wyble, Folk, and Potter, 2013*

New studies show that our brains process and interpret videos incredibly quickly, far faster than we do language. Gestalt psychology points to the unconscious influence visuals have on our minds.

*The Picture Superiority effect allows us to understand and remember more accurately. In one study, participants were over 90% accurate in a recognition test several days later.*

*Standing, Conezio, & Haber, 1970*

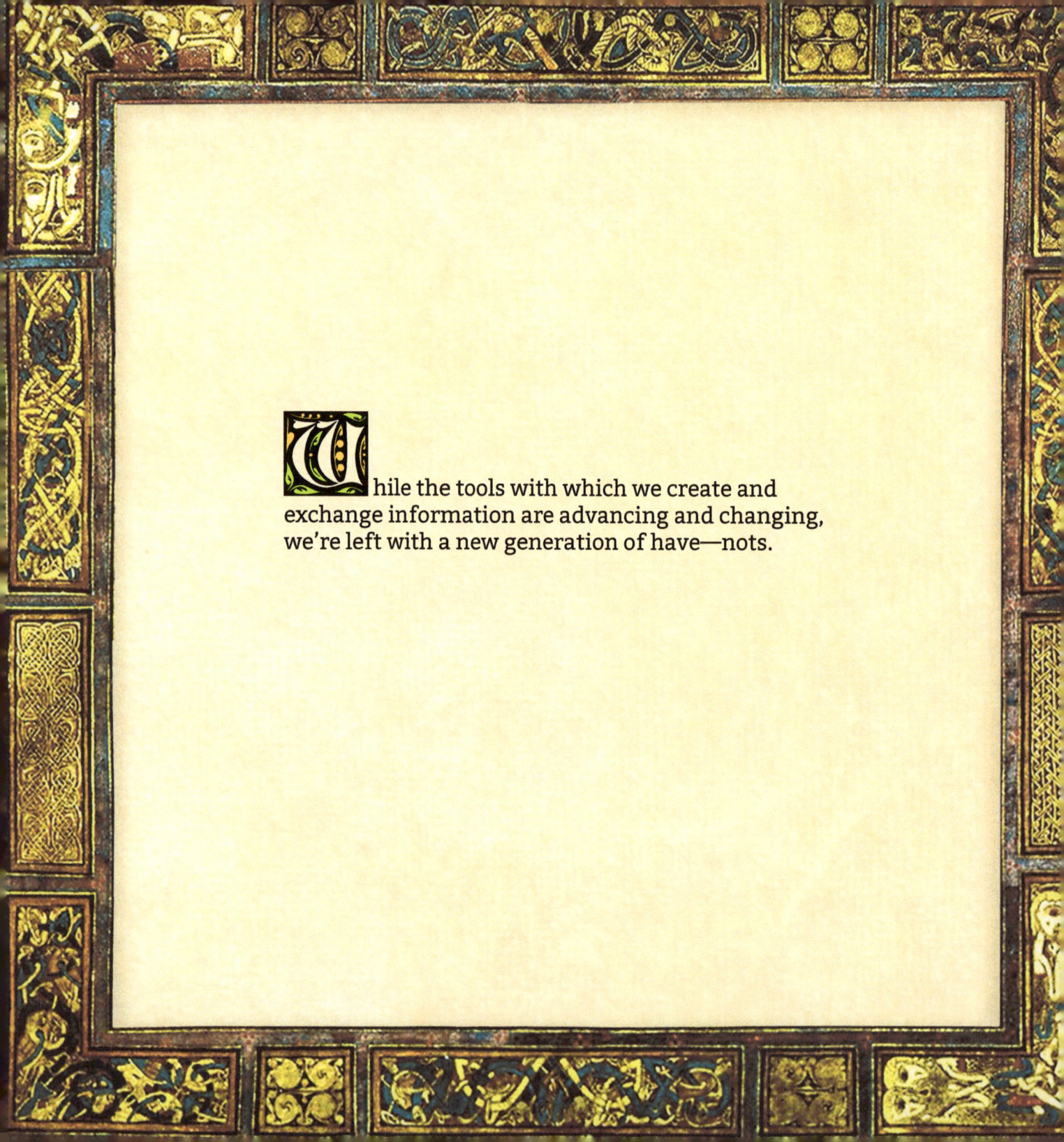

While the tools with which we create and exchange information are advancing and changing, we're left with a new generation of have—nots.

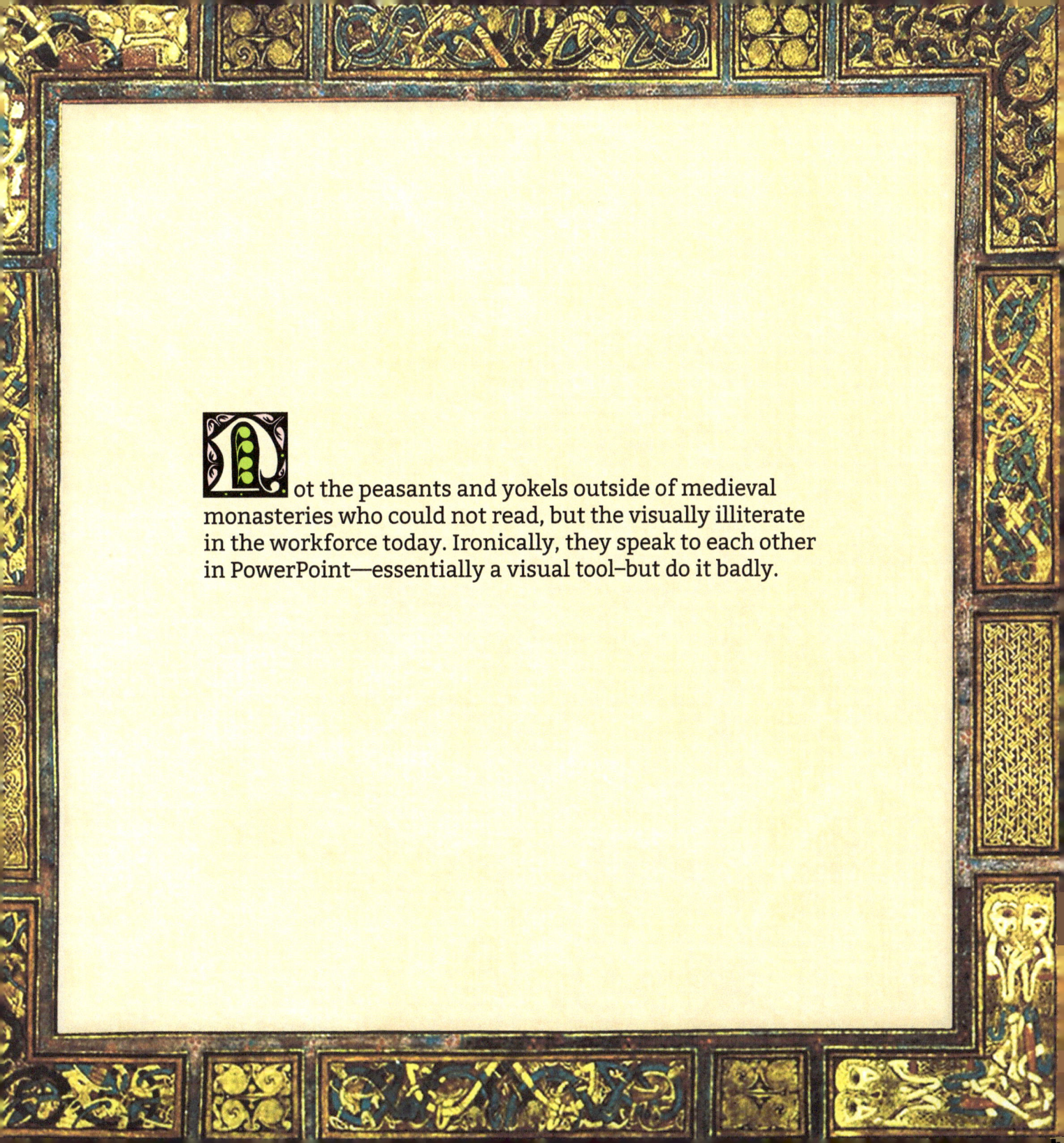

**N**ot the peasants and yokels outside of medieval monasteries who could not read, but the visually illiterate in the workforce today. Ironically, they speak to each other in PowerPoint—essentially a visual tool–but do it badly.

# Conversations matter.

Correlation between effective communication and...

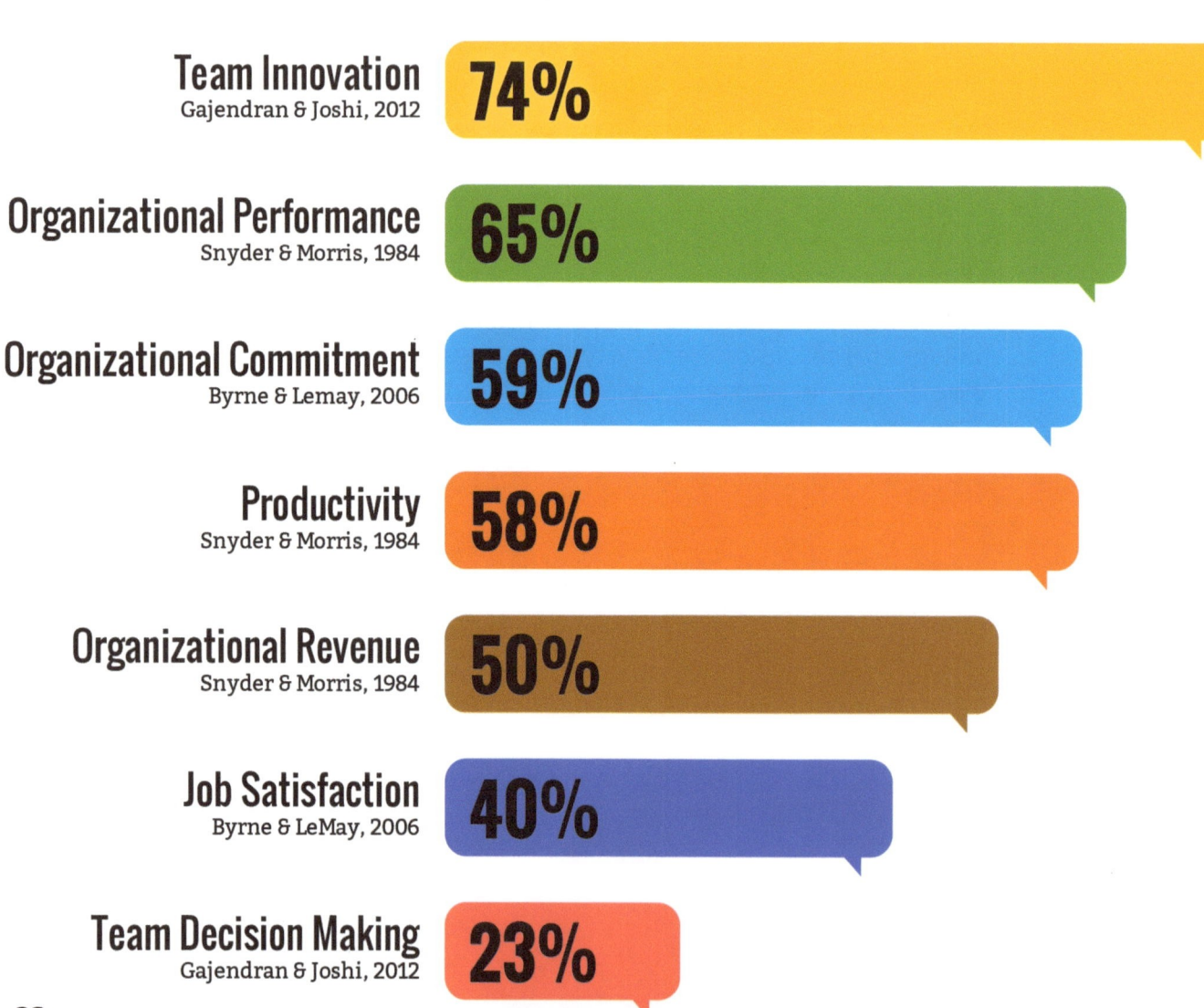

**Team Innovation**
Gajendran & Joshi, 2012
**74%**

**Organizational Performance**
Snyder & Morris, 1984
**65%**

**Organizational Commitment**
Byrne & Lemay, 2006
**59%**

**Productivity**
Snyder & Morris, 1984
**58%**

**Organizational Revenue**
Snyder & Morris, 1984
**50%**

**Job Satisfaction**
Byrne & LeMay, 2006
**40%**

**Team Decision Making**
Gajendran & Joshi, 2012
**23%**

Millions of PowerPoints are produced every day and business has made it its Lingua Franca, though most just add to the noise. And it's not just PowerPoint; we've invented new categories like infographics, data visualization and "explainer" videos, all of which leave a lot to be desired.

# IF YOU HAVE READ THIS FAR, CONGRATULATIONS YOU'RE LITERATE.

Reading and writing are essential skills in life and business. The great leaders of the last century had a command of language and turn of phrase that allowed them to persuade, convince and cajole. But is your literacy enough? Does your message get through? Are people paying attention to what you have to say, or what you have to sell? What do you do if you're of a generation that's literate, but not visually literate? If you're one of those people that has to get a message out and through, can you keep it from being swallowed by all the noise?

The generation that follows yours will be digitally native *and* visually literate. Will you be able to compete?

If your answer is no, maybe, or a hesitant yes, consider what visuals and visual literacy can do for you. They can help frame your message and move people to action. They can simplify and explain your ideas. They can add riches to your story.

You are a NASA scientist and need to **inform** us that a comet is hitting Jupiter.

You are the head of HR and need to **instruct** employees on how to enroll in the new insurance plan.

You're delivering a talk on reducing stress in the workplace, add an **entertaining** slant to it.

You're role is to **inspire/motivate** a sales group by sharing a story of overcoming a tragedy in life.

You need to **stimulate** a crowd to take action and give large donations for a new hospital wing.

You need to **persuade** your largest prospect to approve the proposal on the table to close down the deal.

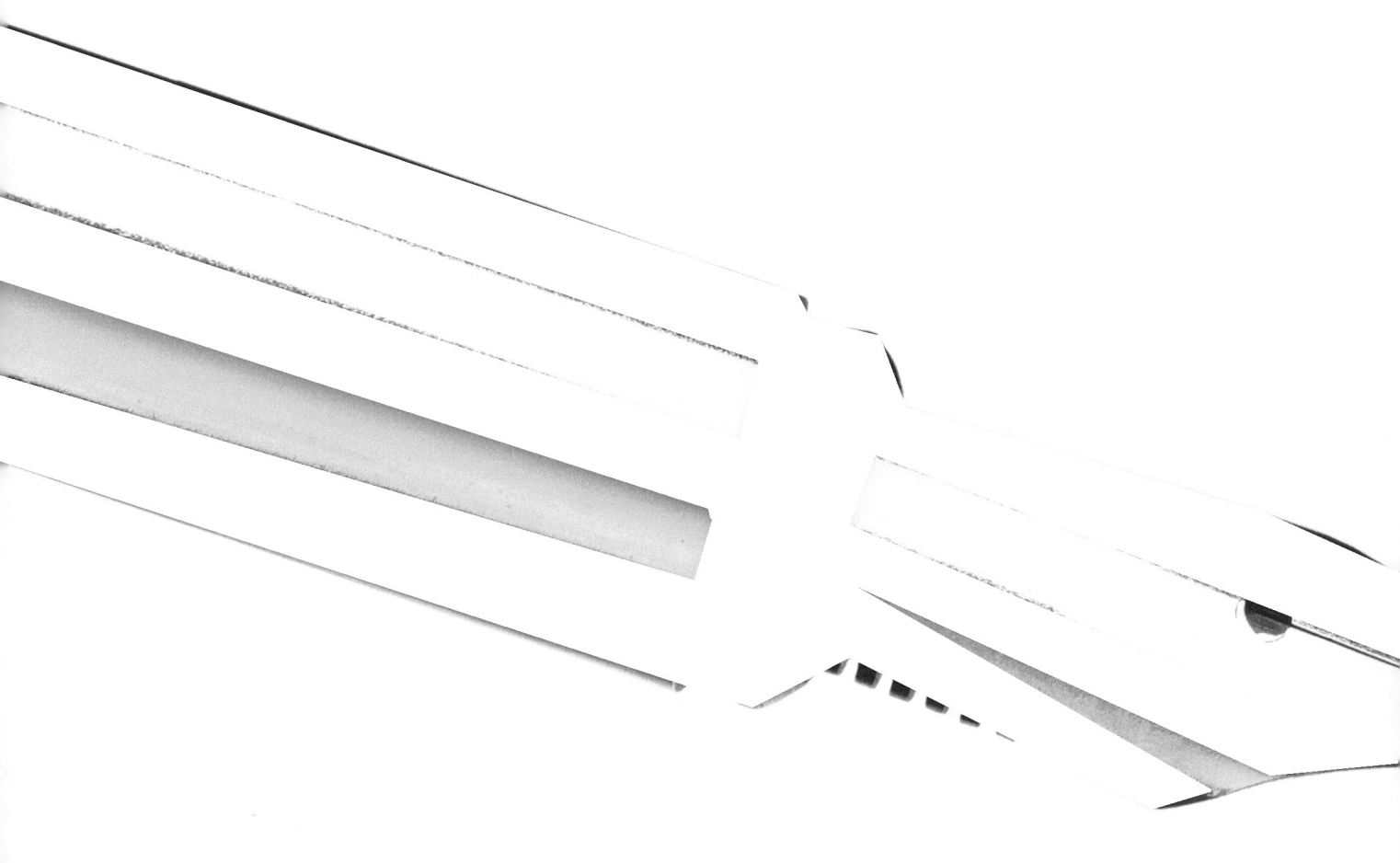

# DOES YOUR MESSAGE GET THROUGH?

www.ingramcontent.com/pod-product-compliance
Lightning Source LLC
Chambersburg PA
CBHW050906180526
45159CB00007B/2805